EMPOWERING MANTRAS
FOR AWESOME
WOMEN

EMPOWERING
MANTRAS
FOR AWESOME
WOMEN

CICO BOOKS
LONDON NEW YORK

This edition published in 2020 by CICO Books
An imprint of Ryland Peters & Small Ltd
20–21 Jockey's Fields   341 E 116th St
London WC1R 4BW   New York, NY 10029

www.rylandpeters.com

10 9 8 7 6 5 4 3

First published in 2018
Design © CICO Books 2020
For photography credits, see pages 143–144.

A CIP catalog record for this book is available from
the Library of Congress and the British Library.

ISBN: 978-1-78249-853-7

Printed in China

MIX
Paper from
responsible sources
FSC® C106563

Designer: Paul Tilby
Commissioning editor: Kristine Pidkameny
Senior editor: Carmel Edmonds
Art director: Sally Powell
Production manager: Gordana Simakovic
Publishing manager: Penny Craig
Publisher: Cindy Richards

INTRODUCTION

This brilliant collection of wise and powerful words is a must-have for any 21st-century woman. Whether you want a reminder of your worth, a boost towards smashing boundaries and glass ceilings, or simply a hit of positivity, you'll find your inspiration here.

Among motivational mantras to shift your mind-set, you'll also discover the sage words of women who shaped history—from abolitionists Harriet Beecher Stowe and Harriet Tubman and suffragist Elizabeth Cady Stanton to novelists such as Charlotte Brontë and Jane Austen and poets such as Emily Dickinson and Christina Rossetti.

You might like to choose a mantra or quotation each morning and keep it in your mind as you face the day's challenges. Try copying words that have particularly resonated with you into your journal, or pin them up around your home or workplace to inspire you. You could even send your favorite words to a friend to help her find her inner strength.

Remember: you are the heroine of your life.

HERE'S TO STRONG WOMEN. MAY WE KNOW THEM. MAY WE BE THEM. MAY WE RAISE THEM

FIND
THE
WONDER
WOMAN
INSIDE
YOU

YOUR MIND HAS THE POWER
AND YOUR HEART WILL
FIND THE WAY

BEAUTY BEGINS THE MOMENT YOU DECIDE TO BE YOURSELF.

Coco Chanel

KNOW THE VALUE OF KNOWING YOUR VALUE

INHALE
CONFIDENCE,
EXHALE
DOUBT

LITTLE GIRLS
WITH DREAMS
BECOME WOMEN
WITH VISION

HEAR
ME
ROAR

DIAMONDS

Adventures

**ADVENTURES
ARE FOREVER**

NEXT TO TRYING AND WINNING, THE BEST THING IS TRYING AND FAILING.

L.M. Montgomery

NEVERTHELESS, SHE PERSISTED

SHE
BELIEVED
SHE
COULD
SO SHE
DID

REMEMBER
YOU ARE
ADORED

BE FEARLESS
TAKE
ACTION

I AM
AT HOME
IN MY
PERSONAL
STORY

YOU HAVE WITHIN YOU
THE STRENGTH,
THE PATIENCE,
AND THE PASSION
TO REACH FOR THE STARS
TO CHANGE THE WORLD.

Harriet Tubman

STEP
INTO YOUR
POWER

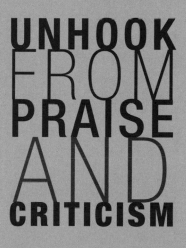

UNHOOK FROM PRAISE AND CRITICISM

BE YOUR OWN BEST FRIEND

CHOOSE COURAGE OVER COMPROMISE

ARE YOU IN?

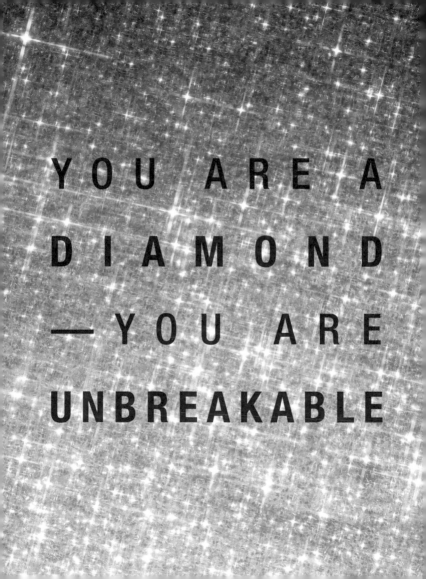

YOU ARE A DIAMOND — YOU ARE UNBREAKABLE

BE DARING

MY WOMAN IS TO STAND ALONE,
AND HELP HERSELF... STRONG-
MINDED, STRONG-HEARTED, STRONG-
SOULED, AND STRONG-BODIED.

Louisa May Alcott

LET GO OF
EXPECTATIONS
AND STAY
CURIOUS

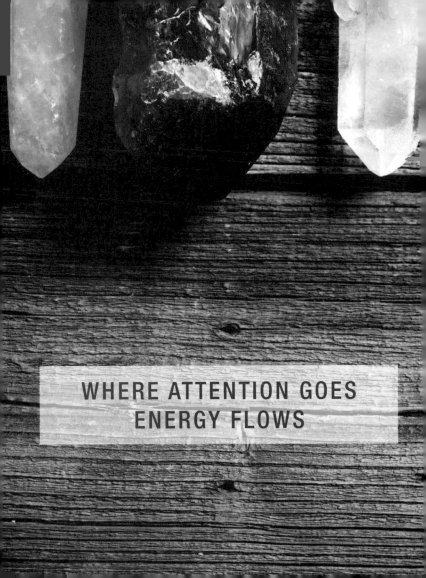

WHERE ATTENTION GOES
ENERGY FLOWS

YOU HAVE AN APPOINTMENT WITH LIFE

COME INTO FULL VIEW

LET'S TAKE UP MORE SPACE

IF YOU LOOK THE RIGHT WAY,
YOU CAN SEE THAT THE WHOLE
WORLD IS A GARDEN.

Frances Hodgson Burnett

THERE IS A STUBBORNNESS ABOUT ME
THAT NEVER CAN BEAR TO BE FRIGHTENED
AT THE WILL OF OTHERS. MY COURAGE ALWAYS RISES
AT EVERY ATTEMPT TO INTIMIDATE ME.

Jane Austen

ONE CANNOT CONSENT TO CREEP WHEN ONE HAS AN IMPULSE TO SOAR.

Helen Keller

EUROPE
IN 1519

**DO
WHAT
YOU
LOVE**

NO ONE CAN MAKE YOU FEEL INFERIOR WITHOUT YOUR CONSENT

Eleanor Roosevelt

SILENCE
IS NOT AN
OPTION

THE BEST PROTECTION ANY WOMAN CAN HAVE ... IS COURAGE.

Elizabeth Cady Stanton

STOP
WISHING.
START
DOING

I AM NO BIRD; AND NO NET
ENSNARES ME; I AM A FREE
HUMAN BEING WITH AN
INDEPENDENT WILL.

Charlotte Brontë

BE
BOLD
AND
BRAVE

WOMEN ARE THE REAL
ARCHITECTS OF SOCIETY.

Harriet Beecher Stowe

TRUST
YOUR
INTUITION

SPEAK THROUGH YOUR LIFE.
YOU WILL CHANGE LIVES

I WANT TO SING LIKE BIRDS SING.
NOT WORRY WHO LISTENS OR
WHAT THEY THINK.

Rumi

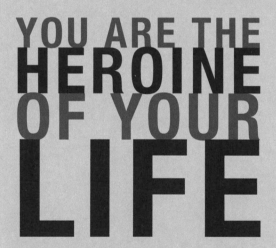

THE MOST EFFECTIVE WAY TO DO IT, IS TO DO IT.

Amelia Earhart

I DO NOT WISH WOMEN TO
HAVE POWER OVER MEN;
BUT OVER THEMSELVES.

Mary Wollstonecraft

ANSWER THE CALL

BE YOUR OWN KIND
OF BEAUTIFUL

I ALLOW SHE HAS
SMALL CLAIMS
TO PERFECTION;
BUT THEN, I IMAGINE
THAT, IF SHE WERE
MORE PERFECT,
SHE WOULD BE
LESS INTERESTING.

Anne Brontë

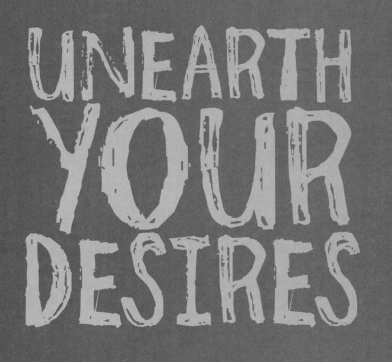

I HATE TO HEAR YOU
TALKING AS IF WOMEN
WERE ALL FINE LADIES,
INSTEAD OF RATIONAL
CREATURES. WE NONE OF
US EXPECT TO BE IN
SMOOTH WATER
ALL OUR DAYS.

Jane Austen

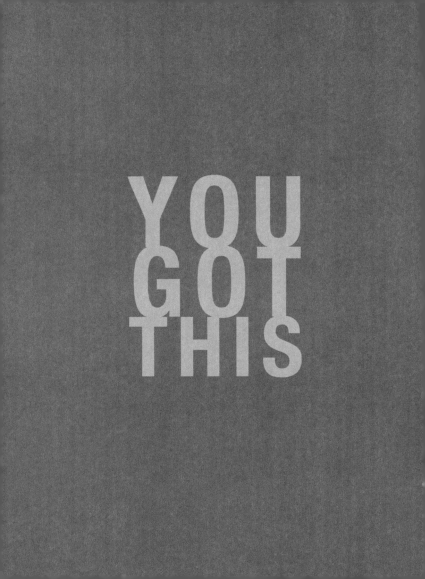

DON'T WAIT FOR SOMEONE TO GIVE YOU PERMISSION

THE BEGINNING IS ALWAYS TODAY

Mary Shelley

I WOULD ALWAYS RATHER BE
HAPPY THAN DIGNIFIED.

Charlotte Brontë

FOR THERE IS NO FRIEND LIKE A SISTER
IN CALM OR STORMY WEATHER;
TO CHEER ONE ON THE TEDIOUS WAY,
TO FETCH ONE IF ONE GOES ASTRAY,
TO LIFT ONE IF ONE TOTTERS DOWN,
TO STRENGTHEN WHILST ONE STANDS.

Christina Rossetti

IN THE WAVES OF CHANGE,
WE FIND OUR TRUE DIRECTION

DO WHAT THEY THINK
YOU CAN'T DO

DON'T
STOP
UNTIL
YOU'RE
PROUD

I'M NOT A PRINCESS
WHO NEEDS TO BE SAVED
—I'M A QUEEN

THE
FUTURE
IS
FEMALE

AND THOUGH
SHE BE BUT
LITTLE,
SHE IS
FIERCE

William Shakespeare

I CONNECT

WITH

MY

TRUE

SELF

AND, OF COURSE, MEN KNOW
BEST ABOUT EVERYTHING,
EXCEPT WHAT WOMEN
KNOW BETTER.

George Eliot

PUT ON
YOUR
LIPSTICK
AND FACE
THE DAY

DARE TO BE
YOUR OWN
ILLUMINATION

WE KNOW WHAT WE ARE, BUT KNOW NOT WHAT WE MAY BE

William Shakespeare

I AM NOT AN ANGEL, AND I
WILL NOT BE ONE TILL I DIE:
I WILL BE MYSELF.

Charlotte Brontë

I AM NOT
AFRAID;
I WAS
BORN
TO DO THIS.

Joan of Arc

TRUTH IS POWERFUL AND IT PREVAILS.

Sojourner Truth

I MATTER EQUALLY

YOU ARE ASTONISHING

INVITE THE MAGIC IN

IT IS NOT EASY TO BE A PIONEER —BUT OH, IT IS FASCINATING!

Elizabeth Blackwell

DON'T SAY
"I CAN'T DO IT."

SAY "I CAN'T
DO IT YET."

WHAT'S YOUR SUPERPOWER?

EMPOWERED
WOMEN
EMPOWER
WOMEN

THE POWER IS IN YOUR HANDS

I'M NOT AFRAID OF STORMS, FOR I'M LEARNING HOW TO SAIL MY SHIP.

Louisa May Alcott

WE NEVER KNOW
HOW HIGH WE ARE
TILL WE ARE
CALLED TO RISE;
AND THEN, IF WE
ARE TRUE TO PLAN,
OUR STATURES
TOUCH THE SKIES.

Emily Dickinson

PROVE
THEM
WRONG

YOU

ARE

GOOD

ENOUGH

SELF-CONFIDENCE

IS THE

BEST OUTFIT

MAKE NO APOLOGIES
FOR WHO YOU ARE

AT FIRST PEOPLE REFUSE TO
BELIEVE THAT A STRANGE NEW
THING CAN BE DONE, THEN THEY
BEGIN TO HOPE IT CAN BE DONE,
THEN THEY SEE IT CAN BE DONE—
THEN IT IS DONE AND ALL THE
WORLD WONDERS WHY IT WAS
NOT DONE CENTURIES AGO.

Frances Hodgson Burnett

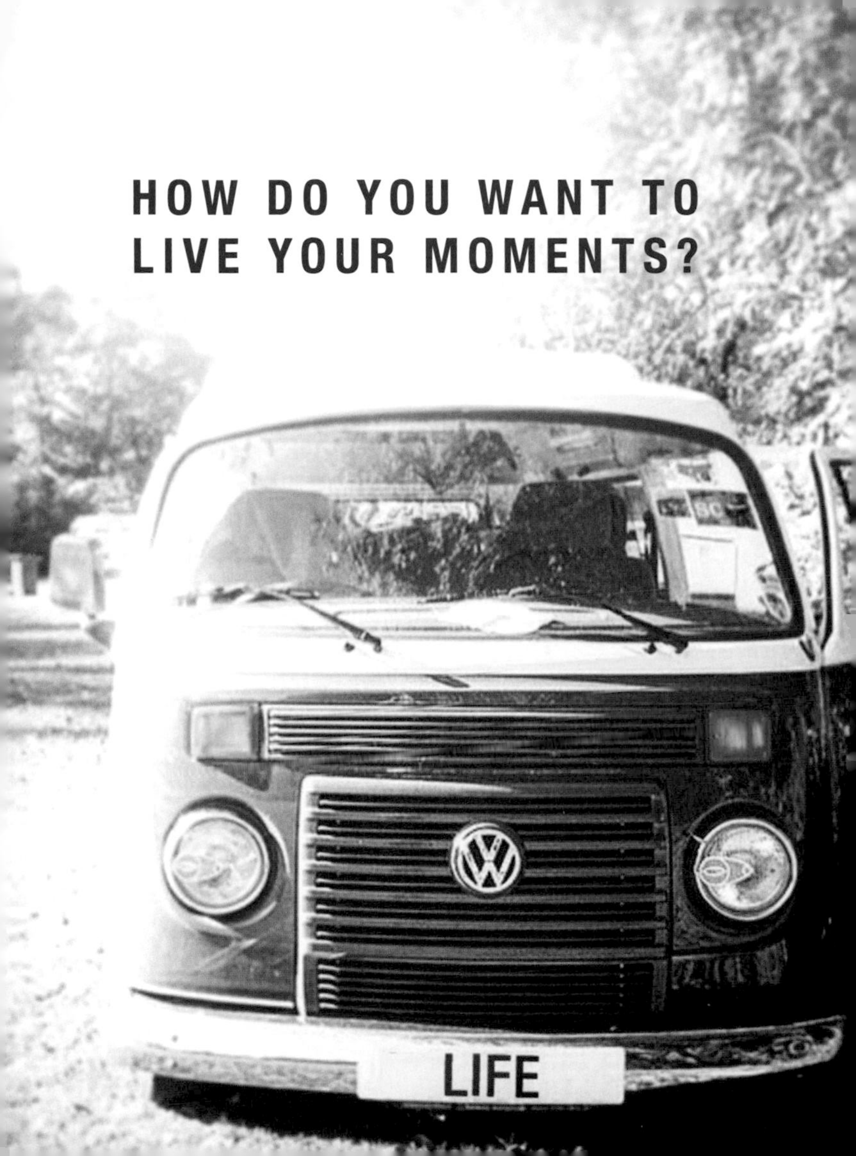
HOW DO YOU WANT TO
LIVE YOUR MOMENTS?
LIFE

I AM STRONG
I AM POWERFUL
I AM A WOMAN

PHOTOGRAPHY CREDITS

KEY: *ph* = photographer